Meg and Rat

and

Puff! Puff! Puff!

D0492407

'Meg and Rat' and 'Puff! Puff! Puff!'
An original concept by Cath Jones
© Cath Jones

Illustrated by Adam Pryce

Published by MAVERICK ARTS PUBLISHING LTD

Studio 3A, City Business Centre, 6 Brighton Road,

Horsham, West Sussex, RH13 5BB

© Maverick Arts Publishing Limited July 2017

+44 (0)1403 256941

A CIP catalogue record for this book is available at the British Library.

ISBN 978-1-84886-286-9

www.maverickbooks.co.uk

This book is rated as: Pink Band (Guided Reading)
This story is decodable at Letters and Sounds Phase 2.

Meg and Rat

and

Puff! Puff! Puff!

By
Cath Jones

Illustrated by
Adam Pryce

The Letter R

Trace the lower and upper case letter with a finger. Sound out the letter.

Down,
up,
around

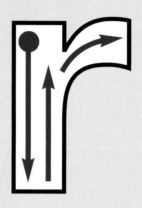

Down,
up,
around,
down

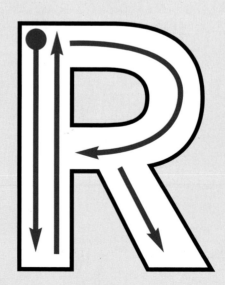

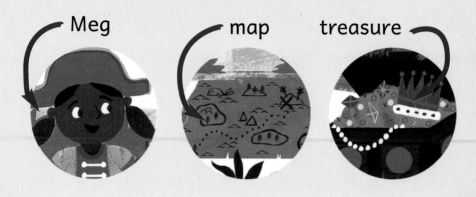

Meg   map   treasure

High-frequency words:

has got a big no the

Tips for Reading 'Meg and Rat'

- Practise the words listed above before reading the story.

- If the reader struggles with any of the other words, ask them to look for sounds they know in the word. Encourage them to sound out the words and help them read the words if necessary.

- After reading the story, ask the reader who finds the treasure at the end.

Fun Activity

Have your very own treasure hunt!

Meg and Rat

Meg has got a big rat.

Meg has got a big map.

Has Meg got a big map?

No!

Has Meg got a big rat?

No!

The rat has got the big map.

The rat has got the treasure!

The Letter F

Trace the lower and upper case letter with a finger. Sound out the letter.

*Around,
down,
lift,
cross*

*Down,
lift,
cross,
lift,
cross*

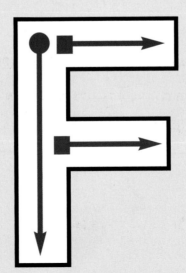

Some words to familiarise:

puff   dog   hen

High-frequency words:

is   a   big   up

Tips for Reading 'Puff! Puff! Puff!'

- *Practise the words listed above before reading the story.*
- *If the reader struggles with any of the other words, ask them to look for sounds they know in the word. Encourage them to sound out the words and help them read the words if necessary.*
- *After reading the story, ask the reader what happens when all the animals have blown up their balloons.*

Fun Activity

Blow up some balloons of your own!

Puff! Puff! Puff!

Nat is a big bat.

NAT

Puff! Puff! Puff!

Pat is a big rat.

Puff! Puff! Puff!

Jen is a big hen.

Puff! Puff! Puff!

Matt is a big cat.

Puff! Puff! Puff!

Mog is a big dog.

Up,

up, up!

Book Bands for Guided Reading

The Institute of Education book banding system is a scale of colours that reflects the various levels of reading difficulty. The bands are assigned by taking into account the content, the language style, the layout and phonics.

Maverick Early Readers are a bright, attractive range of books covering the pink to purple bands. All of these books have been book banded for guided reading to the industry standard and edited by a leading educational consultant.

For more titles visit:
www.maverickbooks.co.uk/early-readers

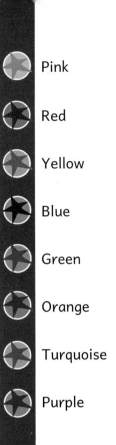

Pink

Red

Yellow

Blue

Green

Orange

Turquoise

Purple

Book Band Pink

Bad Dog and No, Nell, No!	978-1-84886-287-6
Meg and Rat and Puff! Puff! Puff!	978-1-84886-286-9
Ned in Bed and Fun at the Park	978-1-84886-285-2
Cool Duck and Lots of Hats	978-1-84886-249-4
Peck, Hen, Peck! and Ben's Pet	978-1-84886-248-7